MO DATA MANAGEMENT

Finding the Value in your

Organization's Most

Important Asset

first edition

Peter Aiken, PhD,

Virginia Commonwealth University

Data Blueprint

with

Juanita Walton Billings, MS/IS,OfficeWorks

Published by:
Technics Publications, LLC
2 Lindsley Road
Basking Ridge, NJ 07920
U.S.A.
http://www.TechnicsPub.com
Edited by Carol Lehn
Cover design by Mark Brye

ISBN, print ed.   978-1-935504-66-5
ISBN, Kindle ed. 978-1-935504-67-2
ISBN, ePub ed.   978-1-935504-68-9

First Printing 2013

Library of Congress Control Number: 2013949392

We would like to dedicate this book to our friend and colleague, Micheline Casey, Chief Data Officer of the Federal Reserve Board and one of the most verifiably experienced CDOs. We look forward to her writing a book in the near future about her experiences as the first state Chief Data Officer and the first CDO at the Federal Reserve Bank.

Table of Contents

List of Figures

Acknowledgements

The first author gratefully thanks the second author for our terrific discussions across the various issues. The exchanges were among the best in my professional career and I gratefully acknowledge the substantive revisions, enhancements and extensions of my original remarks. I also want to thank my friend and colleague Joseph Cipolla. In our numerous joint lectures to our various MBA classes Joe has never let me forget that when speaking with executives, you must use their language and that this ultimately involves numbers and usually money!

The second author returns thanks to the first for the many opportunities to collaborate over the years and especially for the continual mentoring that has been her pleasure to share with her clients throughout her professional career.

We both thank profoundly Linda Bevolo who jumped in with her contribution just as this book was going through its final revisions and John Bottega who took time out of his very busy schedule to both review the book and write the foreword.

We both acknowledge the hundreds of data managers with whom we have worked over the past two decades. Your stories and success have been a constant source of ideas for us. Here's hoping you will find some inspiration to create your own monetizing data management stories and, in the process, help your bosses better understand the importance of what you do for them and their organizations.

About the Authors

Peter Aiken is acknowledged to be a top data management authority. As a practicing data manager, consultant, author, and researcher, he has been actively attempting to improve this area for more than 25 years. His expertise has been sought by some of the world's most important organizations, and his achievements have been recognized internationally. In addition to examining more than 500 data management practices, he has spent multi-year immersions with organizations as diverse as the US DoD, Deutsche Bank, Nokia, Wells Fargo, and the Commonwealth of Virginia. As President of DAMA International (dama.org), his practice leadership is unquestioned. He has been a member of the Information Systems Department at Virginia Commonwealth University's Business School since 1993 and jointly owns, with the University, Data Blueprint(.com) an award-winning, data management/information technology consulting firm.

With over 30 years of broad experience in the public, private and academic sectors, **Juanita Walton Billings** is a pragmatic, ISO-certified business professional who specializes in analysis, design and auditing of enterprise architectures. Beginning her career as a clerk-typist for a mortgage banking firm, she worked her way up through positions requiring a more sophisticated and technical skill set. She went on to earn a BBA/MIS at James Madison University and an MS/IS at Virginia Commonwealth University. Employed by CMU/SEI to conduct a comparison of the pivotal Zachman Framework and the then-evolving Department of Defense Architecture Framework, she was introduced to enterprise architecture.

Since then, she has established a proven track record based on experience and knowledge gained at the Office of the Attorney General for the Commonwealth of Virginia and various commands, services and agencies of the Department of Defense, in addition to that acquired in privately held legal, health care, banking, not-for-profit, insurance and bonding, retail and construction organizations. She served on the Department of Defense Data Metamodel working group, and she is a published author as well as a former entrepreneur and instructor in the field of management information systems. She brings hands-on experience in the fields of systems, application and human-computer interface analysis and design, data communications, data engineering, data and systems mapping and modeling, business process analysis, modeling and re-engineering, information system organization and management, gap analysis, requirements management, reverse-engineering, systems conversion, e-business, e-governance, consulting, training, troubleshooting and a keen interest in enterprise architecture to the table when reporting and writing. Her self-proclaimed most-valued professional assets include a keen eye for detail and the ability to act as a bridge between technical staff and business users. Bottom line: It's all about the data.

Contributor Bio: With over 30 years of experience in technology and data management, **Linda Bevolo** is a pro-active, passionate, data professional starting, accelerating or fine-tuning data management programs throughout her career. Linda smiles over the "Data Integrity Queen" title given to her by CEO of SNMC after resolving significant data issues and implementing a data management program. With a diverse background including SVP of Development, Owner of LB Data solutions, USA patent holder, Data Management and Data Architect Manager, Developer, Data Architect and DBA, Linda has seen a 360 view of the data and truly understands how to create a data-centric organization. As president of the DAMA St. Louis Chapter, she strives to bring awareness to the field of data management.

Foreword

It seems that not too long ago, any discussion regarding data management would have invoked one of three reactions: (1) eyes glazed over; (2) a faint recognition of the importance of data management, but little support or investment; or (3) an assumption that data management is a tech-only challenge and should be passed over to technology. Today, things have changed. Businesses large and small, across all industries, are coming to grips with the need to recognize, prioritize and manage data, as one of the most fundamental business assets of their institutions.

What has changed? And what is yet to be understood?

We have seen a dramatic shift towards understanding data as a result of several key events. The financial crisis of 2008 was one such event and a turning point for the data management discipline. Data was not the cause of the crisis, but not being able to aggregate, compare, and truly understand the data that was before us impacted our ability, or the ability of the key decision makers, to react and respond. Imagine the best alarm system in the world installed in your home or office, that when activated, shouted commands to you in a foreign language that you could not understand. All of the data provided by the alarm system would have been correct. The delivery of the data was on time and on spec. But the 'meaning' of the data was missing. And without meaning, without that understanding, your response to the data would have been flawed, resulting in potentially fatal outcomes. The financial crisis brought this reality home. Understanding our data was suddenly promoted from the back office, to the c-suite. Data practices were being discussed in industry, across government agencies, and built into regulations. Data, data standards, and data management could be heard in testimony to Congress! The knock-on effect of not-knowing what our data was telling us became real.

And while events such as this were taking place, data itself was growing. If not understanding our data was bad enough; this same data was multiplying at enormous rates. Systems capturing hundreds of thousands, millions, or billions of events or transactions, are flooding into business systems. Databases are growing, capacity is expanding, but is the know-how to 'understand' and make sense of all this data, keeping pace?

Fair to say, we now know that data is important. We now know that data is critical to our everyday activities. Understanding our data is critical to running our business processes more efficiently, to controlling our costs, to creating better and more innovative products, and to servicing our customers better. But do we really know how to realize the true value of data? Do we really know the monetary impact of our data management decisions (or lack thereof)?

The bottom line is — data is the new currency. Yes, an expression that is being used quite a bit of late, but it is very relevant in discussing the importance of data and the methodologies by which we manage it. And like any currency, how we manage it determines its true value. Like any currency, it can be managed wisely, or it can be managed foolishly. It can be put to good use, or it can be squandered away. The question is — what factors determine the path that we take? How do we properly manage this asset and realize its full value and potential?

In *Monetizing Data Management*, Peter and Juanita explore the question of how to understand and place tangible value on data and data management. They explore this question through a series of examples and real-world use cases to exemplify how the true value of data can be realized. They show how bringing together business and technology, and applying a data-centric forensic approach can turn massive amounts of data into the tools needed to improve business processes, reduce costs, and better serve the customer.

Data monetization is not about turning data into money. Instead, it's about taking information and turning it into opportunity. It's about the need to understand the real meaning of data in order to extract value from it. And it's about achieving this objective through a partnership with business and technology. Data management is not a discipline reserved for technology alone. Data management requires business understanding and an understanding of the subject matter at hand, coupled with innovative and supportive technology, to fully realize the true value of data – to inform, expose, and direct business activity to better serve its intended use. In *Monetizing Data Management*, the authors address these objectives and demonstrate how true value can be realized from our data through improved data centric approaches. Enjoy the read but make use of the examples ...

John Bottega
Chief Data Officer for a large financial institution

Executive Summary

We seriously doubt that anyone would have purchased this book if it were titled: *Leveraging Data Assets to Reduce Organizational Risk,* but that is really what this book is about. More practically, the real title of this short book should be: *Monetizing (and otherwise elevating the importance of) Data Management So It Will Get Some Much Needed Attention in the C-Suite.*

That title is too long because it violates all search engine optimization rules. So, knowing that most C-level conversations eventually turn to money, we opted for the shorter title. However, knowing that some organizations have other top-line motivations, we also included non-monetary examples where data management has saved lives and legal bills – both contributing to the concept of organizational risk.

The concept of data as an asset that should be used to support organizational strategy is not sufficiently well known to those whose job it has become to manage data and organizational assets in general. Supported by our approach to monetizing and otherwise elevating the importance of data management practices, you will recognize the importance of improving the data management within your enterprise and the value of leveraging well-managed data. Not only will you more fully understand how data can be used in innovative ways to achieve strategic objectives, you will also no doubt identify opportunities to eliminate wasted resources and build in productivity advantages.

This book defines the five interrelated best practices that comprise organizational data management, highlighting its importance in today's organizational environment and explaining why it is likely being accomplished less than optimally in your organization.

Further, it describes a value-added approach to managing enterprise resources and assets—a data-centric method that provides opportunities for organizational improvements and inherent pay-offs.

The 17 specific cases (of varying lengths) we relate will help you to identify opportunities to introduce data management into the strategic conversations that occur in the C-suite. You will gain a new perspective regarding the stewardship of your data assets and insulate your operations from the chaos, losses and risks that result from traditional approaches to technology projects. And you will learn how to protect yourself from legal challenges resulting from IT projects gone badly due to incorrect project sequencing and focus. With the emerging acceptance and adoption of revised performance standards, your organization will be better prepared to face the coming *big data deluge!*

This little book emerged from a series of talks given around the world by the authors faced with the task of helping our data management community better articulate the importance of what we do for organizations. After due consideration and much consultation with our peers, the answer became obvious. Until the data management community can meaningfully communicate in monetary or other terms equally important to the C-suite, we will continue to struggle to articulate the value of its role within organizational evolution.

Today's business executives are smart, talented and experienced experts who have done incredible things with their organizations. Unfortunately, they have been taught by our educational system that data management is a technical skill that belongs in the bowels of information technology organizations. This results in executive decision-makers being far removed from day-to-day information, and especially data, operations and, for the most part, being insufficiently data knowledgeable to make good data decisions. Consequently, too many decisions about data have been poor.

We organized the book into four chapters:

- **Chapter 1** gives a somewhat unique perspective to the practice of leveraging data. We describe the motivations and delineate the specific challenges preventing most organizations from making substantial progress in this area.
- **Chapter 2** presents 11 cases where leveraging data has produced positive financial results that can be presented in language of immediate interest to C-level executives. To the degree possible, we have quantified the effect that data management has had in terms that will be meaningful to them also.
- **Chapter 3** describes five instances taken from the authors' experiences with various governmental defense (and defence) departments. The lessons in this section however can be equally applied to many non-profit and non-defense governmental organizations.
- **Chapter 4** speaks specifically to the interaction of data management practices, in terms of both information technology projects and legal responsibilities. Reading it can help your organization avoid a number of perils, stay out of court and better vet contractors, experts and other helpers who play a role in organization information technology development.

This book is, we hope, the answer to a question posed by many following our lectures: "Can you get this information into a form where I can hand it to my boss and ask that it be read on the next plane ride?" So, please hand this to your boss, and let us know whether or not it works. (You can email the first author at peter@datablueprint.com.)

Chapter 1
Data Management as a Prerequisite to Data Leveraging

Chapter 1 frames the context for data management by defining the five interrelated practices that comprise organizational data management, highlighting its importance in today's organizational environment, explaining why it is likely being accomplished poorly in your organization today and describing a better approach—a data-centric approach to technology initiatives that highlights organizational pay-offs. Chapter 1 concludes by introducing our approach to monetizing these practices.

WHAT IS DATA? AN OBJECTIVE DEFINITION

Data represents an organization's sole non-depletable, non-degrading, durable, strategic asset. You can't use it up. If properly maintained, it cannot degrade over time or from use. It is, by accounting definitions, durable—persisting beyond the one-year yardstick applied by standard accounting practices. Data's value increases as it evolves along the information value chain. From business predications, it instantiates into transactions and, ultimately, returns full cycle—becoming the basis for future predications of organizational strategy. So far, we have failed to acknowledge data's primary potential value: fit-for-use factual information that describes an organization's operational environment and improves decision-making. When combined, these attributes render data assets unique within the organizational repertoire. Data assets demand to be managed as professionally and aggressively as any other company asset. Objective measurements show that few organizations achieve data management success, resulting in an inability (or at least great difficulty) to exploit a strategic data advantage. In the face of ongoing data explosion, this leaves most organizations unprepared to properly leverage their data assets.

Figure 1 shows that formal definitions of an organzation's data and information are necessary but insufficient prerequistes to organizational use of information as a strategic asset. The figure is an extension of Appleton's original model [see (Appleton 1986)], specifying the relationships and dependencies between the concepts of INTELLIGENCE, INFORMATION and DATA. The elegance of his original model derives from the pictorial explanation of hierarchical dependencies. An organization's strategic use depends on the information and data layers below. Each layer represents a necessary but insufficient prerequisite to organizational quests to leverage data.

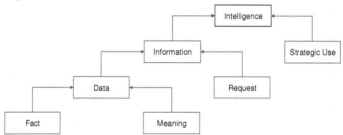

Figure 1   A model showing how data and then information are necessary but insufficient prerequisites to obtaining strategic information use

From the bottom:
1. DATA is a combination of a FACT explicitly paired with one or more MEANINGs. Each FACT combines with one or more MEANINGs. Each specific FACT and MEANING combination is referred to as a *datum*. Data is based on its discrete value and the definition of that value: FACT and MEANING. The formal arrangement of an organization's data assets is referred to as its *data architecture*. All organizations have data architectures; some organizational data architectures are better understood and therefore more useful than other organizations' data architectures.

2. INFORMATION, in turn, is based on the DATA layer and combines specific data with specific REQUESTs. INFORMATION is one or more DATA that is returned in response to a specific REQUEST. To make the most effective use of organizational data and information resources, they must be formally managed. DATA and INFORMATION must be formally arranged into an *architecture*. Incorporation of the various requests is the only thing that differentiates an information architecture from a data architecture. Since the two are intrinsically interrelated, organizations must manage them as one asset—and refer to it as either its data architecture or its information architecture. Attempting to manage them separately causes far more harm than benefit. For this book, we will use the term *data architecture*. *You must select the more appropriate term for your organization and you must train everyone to use the selected term only— not both.* The confusion is not worth the cost.

3. *Information reuse* is enabled when one FACT is combined with more than one MEANING. Information reuse offers far more potential than software reuse – a concept that is largely seen as a failed endeavor.[1] This is attributed to currently unresolved issues with definitions, component classification and existing software development practices. NOTE: these same issues inhibit data reuse, but the challenges are orders of magnitude simpler. And data-focused methods are much more mature.

4. INTELLIGENCE [2] is derived from understanding both information and its associated frame of reference: its

---

[1] Google the phrase "how much software is really reused" and you will find hundreds of reports indicating that the cost of reusing software is now widely perceived as far more expensive than recreating it or purchasing new software packages.

[2] The terms *wisdom* and *knowledge* are often used synonymously.

STRATEGIC USE. INTELLIGENCE is INFORMATION associated with its STRATEGIC USEs. The organizational INTELLIGENCE layer must be developed using specification and common understanding of the subordinate data architecture.

As with any architectural construct, one cannot build a complex, lasting (and hence valuable) structure without a strong foundation. A multi-story house cannot be built upon a base of marshmallows or sand. If the foundation is unable to support higher levels, the entire effort—and structure—will be crippled. The data and information layers are foundational building blocks.

Failure to understand these initial architectural concepts about the relationship between data, information and its strategic use are the primary reason so many organizational business intelligence/ analytical initiatives fail or take longer, cost more, deliver less and present significantly increased organizational risk!

Without diving too deeply into the subject, it should now be obvious that creation of separate piles of business intelligence/ analytical data is counter-productive in most instances – creating duplicate data and wasting effort by cleaning analytical data instead of reforming source data handling practices (to name just one common practice).

The rest of this chapter will address a number of topics somewhat familiar to data managers, but perhaps not as well known to organizational business executives—and especially your C-level executives. We will discuss:

- the engineering and architectural concepts behind data leveraging;
- a formal definition of data management;
- the importance of data management to organizational success;
- the benefits of value-added data management versus traditional data management;

- the need to re-examine information technology support of the business from a data-centric perspective;
- our approach to monetizing data management;
- detailed examinations of five data management practice areas; and
- the critical need to improve organizational data management maturity.

DATA LEVERAGING REQUIRES ARCHITECTURAL AND ENGINEERING DISCIPLINES

Most refer to *management* as being a goal.[3] Management, however, is a necessary (but insufficient) prerequisite to successful data leveraging; leveraging is the higher-order objective. Advantageous data management is a prerequisite to achieving organizational data leverage, that is, strategic use of information. Exploiting a data advantage is what brings recognized value to data assets. Data assets must be perceived holistically and, more importantly, independent of technology—in the same manner in which a chief financial officer understands the available range of financial assets and instruments. The concept, *in support of organizational strategy*, is foreign to those whose job it has become *to manage data*.

Good data management practices must precede effective, innovative organizational data use and, specifically, information technology development projects. Failure to focus on this foundation ensures that value emerging at the intelligence level is diminished as a result of taking longer, costing more, delivering less reliable facts and presenting greater risk to the organization. Poor

---

[3] It is an important goal, consider the question: *"How can you secure it if you can't manage it?"* and associated implications for the information security industry.

data architectural foundations represent a particular threat to the allure of big data leveraging techniques.

The process of building your data architecture must be managed inductively—based on factual information—derived from accurate and timely data that already exists. Such information can be effectively and efficiently extracted using reverse-engineering techniques that have been refined over decades [see (Aiken, Muntz *et al.* 1994)]. When combined with some exciting automated reverse-engineering technologies, [4] organizations can rapidly reclaim mastery of their data assets.

Similarly, without knowledge of the engineering disciplines, it is impossible to effectively leverage data within the organization and among partners. Leverage is achieved using data-centric technologies, processes and human skill sets. Leverage is increased as redundant, obsolete or trivial (ROT) data is eliminated from organizational data (Figure 2).

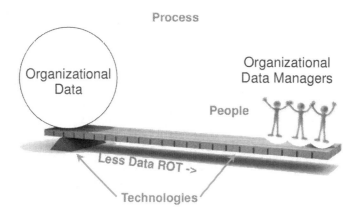

Figure 2   Leverage as an engineering concept – levering effectiveness is increased as data ROT is reduced

---

4   See for example: http://globalids.com

Perceiving and treating data as an asset simultaneously (a) lowers information technology costs and (b) increases knowledge worker productivity.

WHAT IS DATA MANAGEMENT?

Data management is generally a poorly understood concept from all perspectives. It is not taught as part of the vast majority of information technology programs, and therefore most information technology professionals and organizational leaders are *not data knowledgeable*. Since one cannot know what one has not learned, it is unfair to blame knowledge workers or executives for not knowing that data management is crucial to successful implementation of information strategies. Consequently, this condition represents a key constraint to comprehensive organizational strategy implementation. However, any holistic examination of the information technology field will reveal that it is largely about *technology*[5]—not about information. So, we can begin by stating that data management is largely about *putting the "I" back into IT.*

A good place to begin developing an understanding of data management is with the *Data Management Body of Knowledge*, often referred to in the industry as the *DMBOK*. Published by DAMA International[6] in 2009, it is the *de facto* guide to understanding data management – quoting:

Data management is the business function (sic) of planning for, controlling and delivering data and information assets. This function (sic) includes the:
- *disciplines of development, execution and supervision of*

---

[5] Comprising 90% of scientific research and writing.

[6] Data Administration Management Association (dama.org) – DMBOK is available at amazon.com – keywords "DAMA DMBOK."

- *plans, policies, programs, projects, processes, practices and procedures that*
- *control, protect, deliver and enhance the*
- *value of data and information assets.*

Data management is known by many other terms:
- *information management (IM)*
- *enterprise information management (EIM)*
- *enterprise data management (EDM)*
- *data resource management (DRM)*
- *information resource management (IRM)*
- *information asset management (IAM)*

All these phrases are generally synonymous, but this writing will consistently refer to data management. Often the word enterprise is included in the phrase to emphasize the enterprise-wide focus of data management efforts, i.e., enterprise information management or enterprise data management. Enterprise-wide data management is a recommended best practice. However, data management may also be performed effectively in a local context without an enterprise-wide scope or mandate, although with less business benefit.

Data management encompasses tasks commonly referred to as database administration with database design, implementation and production support, as well as data administration. The term data administration was once a popular way to vaguely refer to all the processes of data management—except database administration. However, as the data management process matures, its specific tasks are better understood. The data management process is important to enterprises of all sizes and purposes.

The scope of the data management process and the scale of its implementation vary widely with the size, means and experience of an organization. The nature of the data management process remains the same across organizations, even though implementation details differ widely. (DAMA-International 2009)

The *DMBOK* uses a wheel (Figure 3) to describe 10 data management processes. While this representation does not show that some tasks are optional and some tasks are dependent upon other tasks, it does serve as a useful starting point for an ultimate understanding that (a) these 10 processes are not taught in the vast majority of educational contexts and, thus, (b) require that knowledge workers seek out alternate sources to learn about them. DAMA International is the data management professional organization dedicated to improving the skills—and utilization—of such professionals.

Figure 3   DAMA DMBOK functions

We can safely state that data management is concerned with the development and execution of architectures, policies, practices and procedures in order to manage the information lifecycle needs of an enterprise in an effective manner. Data lifecycle management is a policy-based approach to managing the flow of an information system's data throughout its lifecycle—from creation and initial storage to that time when it becomes obsolete and is deleted. Effective data management involves well-thought-out procedures and adherence to best practices.[7] Further, it is the administrative process by which required data is acquired, validated, stored, protected and processed and by which its accessibility, reliability and timeliness is ensured to satisfy the needs of the data user.[8]

WHY IS DATA MANAGEMENT IMPORTANT?

Data management improves organizational effectiveness in two primary ways.

- **Too much data leads directly to wasted productivity.** The primary justification for data management is the fact that eighty percent (80%) of organizational data is redundant, obsolete or trivial (ROT). By taking excessive time to locate data needed to answer specific questions and by negatively impacting information reliability (fitness for use) as a result of poor data quality and calcification resulting from slow response to environmental changes, data ROT impedes and diminishes organizational performance.

- **Underutilized data leads directly to poorly leveraged organizational resources.** Corporate resources are used to satisfy customer demand for acceptable products and services in such a manner as to generate revenues and profits to sustain the business of the enterprise. More simply stated, corporate resources consist of the following

---

[7] Tech Target at http://searchdatamanagement.techtarget.com/definition/data-management

[8] Business Dictionary at http://www.businessdictionary.com/definition/data-management.html

high-level elements, all of which are dependent upon supply and managed by effectiveness and cost:

- **manpower** – costs associated with labor resources and market share
- **money** – costs associated with management of financial resources
- **methods** – costs associated with operational processes and product delivery
- **machines** – costs associated with hardware, software applications and data to enhance production capability.

Manpower (labor) is traditionally the largest cost factor associated with producing a product or service. Often, however, it's the machines that unnecessarily consume a lion's share of the budget. And although many organizations have begun to recognize corporately owned data as an asset, several factors, both direct and indirect, can be blamed for the fact that it continues to be underutilized. More importantly, as a result of the situation, the corporate bottom line continues to feel an unacceptable negative impact. To help you understand, visualize an application of the organizational data management process.

Picture the process of planning a new restaurant. One alternative would be to go with the concept that *presentation* is everything. Each menu item would be served to patrons on a uniquely crafted plate. The apple pie plate might be shaped like an apple while the banana ice cream dish would be banana shaped. As a strategy, this might well reinforce the new restaurant's uniqueness to its customers. However, if the banana ice cream dish was broken during delivery, the cost of locating a new banana shaped dish might be high when compared to the alternative of serving everything using the standard plates. The cost of maintaining an inventory consisting of a large number of different serving plates might be high and would be factored into the planning, as would the costs of organizing the serving dish racks for easy access. Had the restaurant planners initially decided that food delivery speed was a higher priority than presentation: (a) all plates would be the exact same size and all bowls would be the exact same size and (b) that all dinnerware will be the exact same color, minimizing plate and bowl production and organizing costs.

Unfortunately, organizations more often fail to include the cost of maintaining multiple, duplicative data items as part of their strategic calculations. When considering that our research shows that the average organization maintains customer information in 17 source systems,[9] it becomes obvious that both IT and business management fail to give this concept (data planning) the same level of attention that other strategic variables receive. Our research indicates that this can cost organizations up to 40% of total IT expenses.

AN INCORRECT EDUCATIONAL FOCUS

We have been teaching smart people the wrong things for decades now. This strong statement means that the last three generations of STEM,[10] business and information technology leaders have been taught the wrong stuff about data and data management and, as a result, they are simply not qualified to make important decisions about organizational data assets and related matters.

Curricula encompassing computer science, information systems and computer engineering—and STEM in general—typically emphasize how to build new systems. As it turns out, this is a

---

[9] The number 17 is a useful benchmark – if your organization maintains customer location in less than 17 disparate locations, you should report to the C-level that you are above average and ask them if they think that this is the correct number of places to maintain their organizational customer information!

[10] STEM stands for science, technology, engineering and math.

fundamental needs mismatch, especially when it is well understood that 80% of IT costs are spent rebuilding and evolving existing systems and only 20% of costs are spent building and acquiring new systems. The thought of putting fresh graduates on new projects makes this proposition more ridiculous. Clearly, given the poor IT implementation record, only the most experienced professionals should be allowed to participate in new systems development. Further, some educators should be redirected to focus on the real challenge being faced by organizations—that being the evolution of existing data and systems architectures to better support organizational strategy.

Instead of approaching data management as a purely technical discipline, it is also critical to understand it has social (i.e., enterprise-wide) impacts as well. Therefore, it requires a blended social-technical approach. Unfortunately, an understanding of the necessary blended approach is sorely lacking on the part of those who teach it.

LACK OF AGREEMENT OVER WHO IS RESPONSIBLE FOR DATA ASSETS

The information technology and business sectors do not agree regarding the various responsibilities related to data assets. The business sector assumes that data is being competently managed by the IT sector; whereas the IT sector is equally certain that the business sector is responsible. Further, disagreement exists within the IT sector, where it is commonly thought that data should fit into existing systems development lifecycle (SDLC) methods. Development lifecycles create something from nothing, whereas successful organizational data evolution must precede any software development lifecycle activity.

Data evolution is separate from, external to and must precede system development life cycle activities!

Organizations achieve little success when attempting to evolve system with methods designed to create something from nothing. Each activity involves a fundamentally different focus.

If we were in charge of data management, our division of responsibility would be organized with all current data management functions (Figure 3) except for two, DATA DEVELOPMENT and DATABASE OPERATIONS MANAGEMENT, moving out of IT (which manages *machines* and their attendant functions) into the business (which establishes *methods* and their attendant activities). Two business data management tasks, metadata management and data security management, are explicitly shared with IT operational activities. This realignment represents a needed, radical shift in thinking and allocation of resources. This argument is articulated more fully in *The Case for the Chief Data Officer* [see (Aiken and Gorman 2013)].[11]

VALUE-ADDED DATA MANAGEMENT IS DERIVED FROM DATA-CENTRIC DEVELOPMENT BEST PRACTICES

Using two figures developed initially by a colleague,[12] we differentiate between traditional *application-centric* and *data-centric* development strategies in Figures 4 and 5. Figure 4 illustrates application-centric development—the strategy used by a vast majority of organizations.

From the top:
- In support of an identified strategy (for example: *Make insanely great products!*), the organization develops specific goals and objectives intended to achieve desired outcomes (for example: *Identify underserved*

---

[11] amazon.com keyword search "AIKEN CDO."

[12] We are indebted to Douglas Bagley (dougbagley73@gmail.com) for this specific conceptualization.

market segments and develop products and services for them).

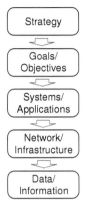

Figure 4　Application-centric development practices

- Next, goals and objectives drive a configuration of specific systems and software applications (for example: *implement operating system "X" installed on server "Y" and purchase software package "Z"*).
- Implementation of those systems and applications leads to network and infrastructure requirements designed to support the configuration (for example: *implement software package "X" using middleware "Y"*).
- Data and information are typically only considered after other design specifications have been articulated (for example: *What data does software package "X" require?*).

Unfortunately, challenges and drawbacks identified with this approach continue to permeate the combined IT/business environment. Processes and data are tightly coupled with applications, making it awkward and costly to maintain or change either the software or the data. Very little data reuse is available with an application-specific focus, and data integrity is at risk. Instead of accommodating organizational information requirements, data requirements are, by necessity, constrained by application requirements.

Figure 5, however, illustrates the fundamental shift in thinking required to first understand and then adopt data-centric development practices. Supporting the notion that business needs (operational processes) should drive system design, the first two steps are common to both figures: determining organizational strategy and specifying specific goals and objectives intended to achieve the strategy. Next, however, a description of information required to achieve measurable goals and objectives is derived from a data architecture that supports organization-wide data usage (for example: *Identify the characteristics, access channels, purchasing power for segments of the product buying public in excess of 100 million potential customers*).

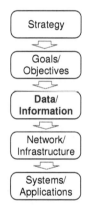

Figure 5   Data-centric development practices differ fundamentally from application-centric development practices

The identified data requirements should be the only variable when determining infrastructure, systems and software package requirements; all other network, software and/or application requirements, then, would be subordinated with delivery platform selection occurring last. In this manner systems and software can be specified and delivered that create the smallest possible footprint while focusing on previously articulated business goals expressed in terms of an organizational data model.

A recent implementation in which we participated involved migration of a large transportation organization from its mainframe because of high costs and structural inflexibility. The organizational decision to adopt our data-centric approach led to an insight that all transactional processing could be done via mobile applications. In turn, this simplified the networking layer to a relatively simple HTTPS implementation. All that was left was a hugely simplified re-skilling of the existing, very competent IT applications group for secure, mobile platform delivery via tablets and the costs of an eight figure implementation was reduced by an order of magnitude!

DATA-CENTRIC APPROACH LEADS DIRECTLY TO ORGANIZATIONAL PRODUCTIVITY ADVANTAGES

When data assets are developed from an organization-wide perspective, systems support organizational data needs complement organizational process flows. Data reuse is maximized. *Situation brittleness*—the ease of breaking a hard-coded condition—can be significantly reduced as a result of separating processes and the data via development of an information architecture. The ability to share and maintain data, *particularly in cases where data is shared across functional areas*, is enhanced. A secondary benefit of shared data is enhancement of data integrity—the accuracy, completeness, timeliness and appropriateness of data. But, because a data-centric approach represents such a fundamental change in organizational thinking, it is generally not on anyone's list of things to monitor. Again, *they do not know what they do not know!*

DATA MANAGEMENT CONSISTS OF FIVE INTEGRATED PRACTICE AREAS

One of the most fundamental missing pieces of knowledge is the actual organization of data management practices. Data management consists of five interrelated specific practice areas (listed and discussed below). Figure 6 shows these as five rounded rectangles and how each is related to the others.[13]

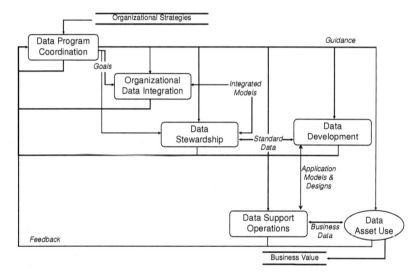

Figure 6   Five integrated data management practices

- **Data Program Coordination** – data management practiced as a coherent and coordinated set of activities aimed at maximizing organizational benefit, specifically, defining, coordinating, resourcing, implementing and monitoring organizational data program strategies, policies, plans etc., as a coherent set of activities:
- **Organizational Data Integration** – delivery of data in support of organizational objectives, specifically, identifying, modeling,

---

13 See Aiken 2007 et al., for more detail.

coordinating, organizing, distributing and designing data shared across business areas or organizational boundaries.

- **Data Stewardship** – designation of specific individuals as caretakers for specific data, ensuring that specific individuals are assigned responsibility for the maintenance of specific data as organizational assets, and that those individuals possess the requisite knowledge, skills and abilities to accomplish these goals in conjunction with other data stewards in the organization.
- **Data Development** – efficient delivery of data via appropriate channels, specifically, specifying and designing appropriately designed data assets that are engineered to be capable of supporting organizational needs.
- **Data Support Operations** – ensuring reliable access to data, specifically, initiation, operation, tuning, maintenance, backup/recovery, archiving and disposal of data assets in support of organizational activities.

IMPROVING ORGANIZATIONAL DATA MANAGEMENT MATURITY

To date, organizations have not proven particularly competent at implementing information technology solutions; minimally, one in three projects (33%) is challenged on price, schedule and ultimate functionality. With more than 25 years of experience in the data management practice, we have observed that the premier shortcoming of organizations conducting information technology assessments and integrations has been a lack of willingness to invest in data management. We have not investigated an IT project failure that didn't ultimately uncover poor data management practices as the root cause of the failure.

Each data management practice area can be objectively quantified using the familiar Carnegie-Mellon University Software Engineering Institute (CMU/SEI) Capability Maturity Model (CMM) scale where scores, increasing from 1 to 5, represent the stage or condition of an organization's data management practices. The CMM levels are:

1. Initial: Our data management practices are ad hoc and dependent upon "heroes" and heroic efforts.
2. Repeatable: We have data management experience and have the ability to implement disciplined processes.
3. Documented: We have standardized data management practices so that all in the organization can perform it with uniform quality.
4. Managed: We manage our data management processes so that the whole organization can follow our standard data management guidance.
5. Optimizing: We have a process for improving our data management capabilities.

A full assessment includes an industry comparison. Figure 7 shows a comparison performed for one of our clients in the airline industry.

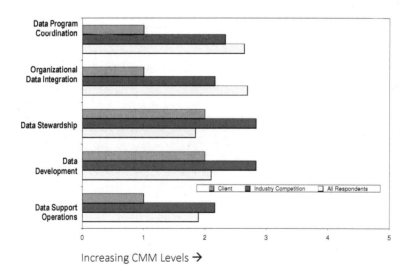

Increasing CMM Levels →

Figure 7   DM Practices within and across industry comparison

Scores for the airline that commissioned the comparison are indicated by the top bars of each group. A "weakest link" scoring system ensures that, since an engineered system can only be as strong as its weakest component, the airline received a score of 1 (the score of the weakest link) based on scores of 1 received on three assessment components.

This particular airline's data management practices were noticeably less mature in the areas of *data program coordination*, *organizational data integration* and *data support*, especially when compared with other airlines that had been assessed. The analysis also indicates that the airline industry (middle bars), was ahead of the general state of the practice (the lowest bars in each group) in some practice areas and behind it in other practice areas.

These results are an extension of the original SEI CMM model. By increasing granularity of the model, organizations can use it as a roadmap indicating that, in this instance, the organization should take steps to enhance maturity of its data management practices by improving its data program coordination, organizational data integration, and data support operations—before attempting to improve the other two practice areas—as these investments will yield a greater ROI than the others.

The objective scores (1-5) shown in Figure 8 can be used to benchmark and monitor industry-wide organizational data management efforts. We have reported on more than 500 organizational surveys and robust empirical measurements that detail the widespread state of data management and the numbers have not statistically varied in this era of big data. Research indicates that, on a scale of 1 to 5 (1 being poor, 5 being outstanding), most organizations are closer to one than to five. This indicates that the average organization *does not employ repeatable data management practice* (Aiken et al. 2007).

Consider the way children benefit from the retelling of stories as a pleasurable pastime, albeit one which builds memory structures. There is a reason that we crawl, walk, run—in that order. While we can't certify that organizations learn in the same manner as humans, there is a parallel. Until an organization gets good at data management, it cannot hope to achieve acceptable results from— or sufficient proficiency at—conducting advanced data practices such as big data techniques, predictive analytics, or even basic data mining.

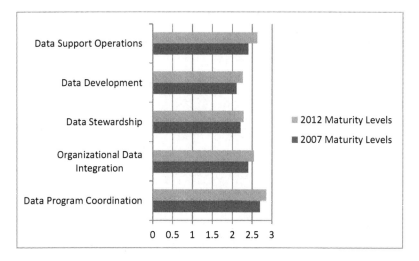

Figure 8   Comparison of industry wide data management maturity levels since dawning of the era of big data techniques (Aiken, Gillenson et al. 2011)

This is best understood by comparing data management practices to Maslow's hierarchy of needs. As shown in Figure 9, advanced data practices occupy the top of the hierarchy. We call them *silver bullets* because they are sold to corporate chief officers (referred to as *C-levels*) as solutions that will solve their problems. (For example, just purchase a solution in the top triangle of Figure 9 and your data problems will vanish.) Most organizations install these solutions with the same competence that they bring to other information technology solutions—that is to say, not much. So a poorly implemented system is then operated by an organization not equipped with sufficient knowledge, skills or abilities. Typically, these "solutions" become shelf ware or otherwise fail to deliver promised benefits.

Figure 9   Basic Data Management Practices prevent organizations from spending too much, experiencing delays, falling short of objectives, and experiencing increased risk

Most organizations fail at data endeavors because they attempt the really cool stuff with data—such as advanced analytics, business intelligence, data warehousing, master data management, big data (the list goes on and on)—before they gain proficiency in the five basic data management practice areas. If you are developing a data warehouse, or any other data-centric information technology system, and if you have not gotten the basics down, it will cost more, take longer and the organization will incur greater risk. Bottom line: does it make sense that the *cost of correction should exceed the cost of the adjustment*?

DATA MANAGEMENT PAY-OFFS

Improving data management practices and the resulting capabilities adds value not only to the information produced, but also to overall organizational goals. Widespread benefits accrue to the entire organization by:

1. helping organizations prepare for future change by implementing a flexible and adaptable organizational data architecture;
2. focusing data assets to efficiently and effectively support organizational strategy;
3. increasing the percentage of time available to accomplish this by lowering the percentage of time required for maintenance activities;
4. reducing organizational data ROT;
5. permitting remaining data to receive more attention with respect to quality, security and reuse;
6. reducing the amount and complexity of the organizational code-base;
7. reducing the amount of time, effort and risk associated with information technology projects;
8. engineering flexibility and adaptability into data architectures instead of attempting to retrofit them after they are in production;
9. producing more, reusable data-focused work products;
10. permitting organizations, when faced with a choice between chaos versus understanding, to gravitate toward a cheaper, more understandable solution;
11. permitting organizations, when faced with a choice between complexity versus ease of implementation, to gravitate toward a cheaper, more understandable solution;
12. decreasing time spent understanding versus time spent considering the data-focused portions of organizational strategy; and
13. minimizing uncertain benefits versus engineerable benefits.

BOTTOM LINE: Data management will, at a minimum, positively impact organizational resources with regard to:
   a. solution development costs related to operations and maintenance time and efficacy,
   b. labor resources required for trouble-shooting and rework,

c. improved data quality and resultant decision-making accuracy and speed, and

d. decreased risk associated with untimely, misguided information.

Unfortunately, sometimes, about the best that can be done is to estimate (and usually, under-estimate) the cost of individual participation in operational processes. That said, this nevertheless permits incorporation of a wider variety of cost modeling and remedial techniques within analysis efforts. Activity-based costing is just one of many measurement techniques available to evaluate data when communicating the leverage possible with advantageous data management. (For further information about this subject, we invite you to read *How to Measure Anything: Finding the Value of Intangibles in Business* by Douglas W. Hubbard, ISBN: 0470539399.) Personally, we were introduced to these techniques when working for and with the US Defense Department in the early 1990s. Techniques presented in the book were used to approximate various costs and benefits associated with specific information technology investment decisions. More importantly, additional benefit accrued from the focused dialog addressing concrete concepts for increasing the ability to meet organizational needs.

A better understanding of costs associated with the execution of specific tasks (processes), the interactions of the tasks (process design), the automation supporting the tasks (processing) and maintenance of operational models (process maps) will accrue from analysis. The same analysis can also give rise to improvements to each of the cost factors.

According to Wikipedia, activity-based costing "… assigns more indirect costs (overhead) into direct costs compared to conventional costing models." So basically, by totaling the cost of a knowledge worker's time expended, we can approach some—but clearly not all—costs. This will permit statements such as "at least amount x is being spent by this organization for task y."

We have used this basic approach for the past 20 years to calculate the minimal costs associated with poor data implementation and presented our calculations in the various cases presented in this book to illustrate to management the tangible costs associated with these decisions.

Chapter 2
Bottom Line Pay-offs: Eleven Financial Cases

Chapter 2 describes eleven cases with specific quantifiable results illustrating how the practice of monetizing data management directly helped a number of organizations in tangible ways that were easy to relate to those in the C-suites. After all, these c-level executives are smart and, when you bring them a plan with good return on investment and results, the next question is usually: where do we go next?

HOW MANY TIMES DO WE HAVE TO SPEND THAT MONEY? ($10 MILLION ANNUALLY)

As part of a state government, all agency employees were required to complete forms that fed the statewide time-and-leave tracking system. For a variety of reasons, the state system often produced information that was both late and inaccurate. Agency employees could not rely on the state's system to meet requirements imposed on them. In typical fashion, the agency developed its own information technology-based, agency-wide time-and-leave tracking system. And surprise, surprise: the agency-level system also produced information that was often both late and inaccurate. But participation in both systems was mandated by various laws and regulations, so each *workgroup* developed a workgroup-based system that satisfied requirements for impromptu weather-based scheduling, something neither of the other two systems could accommodate. Now, you might think we are done here but, wait: *individual workers* maintained a fourth system to assist them with reconciliation of the workgroup solution to the agency- and state-level systems!

It was well understood that every agency employee spent at least 15 minutes each week attempting to maintain accurate individual time-and-leave records. In an attempt to justify development of a statewide solution, our team was assigned the task of documenting every individual who spent more than 15 minutes a week tracking time and leave. So the statement accompanying the chart declared: "At least 300 individuals spend at least 15 minutes per week managing time/leave data." As data was collected, data reflecting pay rank was incorporated (see Figure 10 to appreciate the comprehensiveness of this reference table), thus permitting computation of some of the pay devoted to each individual spending time managing time and leave data. (We couldn't directly identify each employee's specific pay but, knowing a specific grade and using the lowest pay on that grade, we were able to calculate a minimum cost that no one disputed.) The result was a calculation of the minimum amount each district was spending on time- and leave-based data management.

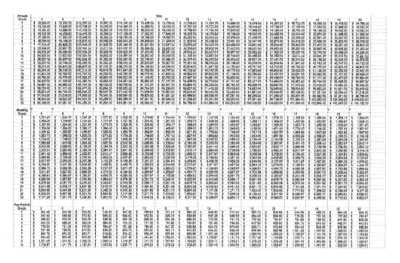

Figure 10   Determining the minimum cost of employee time

In the sample shown (Figure 11), District-L had 73 employees tracking leave and another 50 tracking time. Knowing employee pay grade and the number of time and leave transactions processed twice-monthly, costs per transaction processed were produced. Summing the monthly district totals yielded a total cost of almost $10 million annually! These numbers helped management understand the various costs of things normally considered to be overhead expenditures and permitted them to begin the process of calculating the costs of complying with various regulations. More importantly, the leveraging power of data management was dramatically illustrated with the realization that a *single system* could eliminate 30% of the time required to adequately manage time-and-leave data and impact all 10,000-agency employees. The decision was a real no-brainer investment given that a $300,000 investment would clearly save the agency $10,000,000 annually.

Routine Data Entry		
District-L (as an example)	Leave Tracking	Time Accounting
Employees	73	50
Number of documents	1000	2040
Timesheet/employee	13.70	40.8
Time spent	0.08	0.25
Hourly Cost	$6.92	$6.92
Additive Rate	$11.23	$11.23
Semi-monthly cost per timekeeper	$12.31	$114.56
Total semi-monthly timekeeper cost	$898.49	$5,727.89
Annual cost	$21,563.83	$137,469.40

Figure 11   Minimal cost of activities performed monthly

WHO'S DOING WHAT, AND WHY? ($25 MILLION ANNUALLY)

An international chemical company with more than $1 billion annual sales focused on developing and manufacturing additives to enhance the performance of oils and fuels. To scientifically understand the enhancements to engine performance, such as cleaner burning fuel, more smoothly running engines and longer lasting machines, they were running hundreds of tests annually—with each test costing up to $250,000! Tests were planned and directed by a large staff of chemical researchers and scientists who relied on informal systems to retain facts regarding, for example, what tests were run using what engine and under what conditions. The researchers evolved their own data management processes and, not having any formal education in data management, they did so in a less than optimal manner.

To illustrate the organizational cost of these sub-optimal data management practices, consider that Dr. X (with 10+ years of experience) is paid approximately $100 thousand annually for her services as an employee. As our engineers worked with Dr. X and her colleagues, they were able to document the tasks and the related amount of time spent organizing data in preparation for analysis versus the amount of time actually spent analyzing data. These practices resulted in members of the group spending 80% of their time performing less-valuable data management tasks and only 20% of their time performing the chemical research they were hired to do.

We compiled a chart showing six types of data management challenges encountered by a large number of their most valued knowledge workers: the PhDs in Chemical Engineering:

1. Manual transfer of digital data – numerous instances of highly educated individuals manually transferring digital data from one computing platform to another by rekeying the data (and introducing errors)
2. Manual file movement/duplication – moving individual instances of electronic files (many of them spreadsheets) via disk or USB drive from workstation to workstation
3. Manual data manipulation – various cut/paste /transformations applied without documentation or procedure when files were received from colleagues,
4. Disparate synonym reconciliation – column labels and column values adjustments based not on objective criteria but on subjective comparison by receivers of the files

5. Tribal knowledge requirements – uncountable erroneous tests caused by practically infinite number of requirements, such as "George always forgets to subtract the weight of the container" or "Susie doesn't properly convert between metric and English measurements"

6. Non-sustainable technology – the only database technology used by the department having gone out of business over a decade prior

Referred to as *shadow IT*, such data preparation efforts are, in reality, information technology projects being run external to centralized and authorized organizational information technology. Hence, shadow IT costs are generally unaccounted for, decision-making with regard to shadow IT projects tends to be subjective and these efforts fail to benefit from mature, centrally implemented information technology practices.

Given a $100 thousand annual salary, Dr. X's employer was aghast to discover that 80% of her work hours were spent accomplishing tasks that should have been performed by an individual whose cost was 40% of Dr. X's salary. And this same individual could handle the data management needs for a group of these PhDs, effectively freeing up Dr. X and her colleagues from data management tasks and resulting in tangible savings and greater-than-expected increases in individual, workgroup and organizational productivity.

As an additional bonus, knowledge workers produce more new ideas faster if they are able to maintain a closer, more focused concentration on their basic tasks by reversing the organizing to analyzing ratio described here. And, this list of benefits does not take into account the reduced risk of introducing errors and acting on erroneous information at the individual, workgroup and organizational levels. Integrating existing systems to easily search and find similar or identical tests specifically reduced expenses, improved the client's competitive edge and customer service, increased time savings and improved operational capabilities.

According to our client's internal business case development, the company expects to realize a $25 million gain in the group's productivity each year, thanks to improved data management processes.

THREE ERP CASES THAT ALSO APPLY TO SOFTWARE APPLICATION PACKAGE IMPLEMENTATION

Enterprise resource planning applications (ERPs) have achieved mixed results. Generally, they are perceived as difficult to implement properly. However, if an organization obtains desired efficiencies within five years, the project is considered successful. What follows are three different ERP stories that could also apply to virtually any packaged application (or as it is also known commercial off the shelf—COTS) software.

How much will the data conversion cost? (2 Years and $3,000,000)

The first example helped management understand the unreasonableness of a proposed project plan submitted by consultants on a government project. Figure 12 is a project artifact. The consultants underbid the cost of the data conversion (a common practice), including a laughable amount of time on the proposed project work breakdown structure for a task labeled "data conversion."

Relevant project details illustrated one very specific problem space. At least 683 individual data items on the Payroll side and 1478 on the Personnel side had to be examined and potentially mapped into the target ERP (see Figure 13). The consultant's proposal contained a section addressing this challenge with a two-person-month (40 person-days) resource. Doing the math makes the proposal unrealistic.

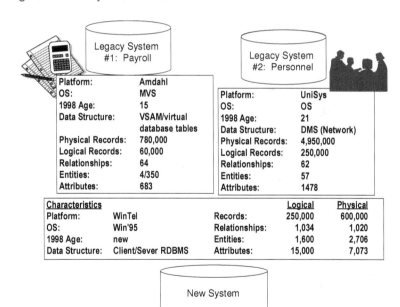

Figure 12   Project estimate

Characteristics			Logical	Physical
Platform:	WinTel	Records:	250,000	600,000
OS:	Win'95	Relationships:	1,034	1,020
1998 Age:	new	Entities:	1,600	2,706
Data Structure:	Client/Sever RDBMS	Attributes:	15,000	7,073

Legacy System #1: Payroll

Platform:	Amdahl
OS:	MVS
1998 Age:	15
Data Structure:	VSAM/virtual database tables
Physical Records:	780,000
Logical Records:	60,000
Relationships:	64
Entities:	4/350
Attributes:	683

Legacy System #2: Personnel

Platform:	UniSys
OS:	OS
1998 Age:	21
Data Structure:	DMS (Network)
Physical Records:	4,950,000
Logical Records:	250,000
Relationships:	62
Entities:	57
Attributes:	1478

New System

Figure 13   Counting data items to be converted

To map 2,161 attributes to 15,000 other attributes would require analysis rates of, on the:

- source side: 2,000/40 person-days = 50 attributes/person-day, and

- target side: 15,000/40 person-days = 375 attributes/person-day.

Adding the two factors yielded a requirement for these individuals to understand and handle 425 attributes every day for 40 days. The true impact of this requirement became obvious with the understanding that the data conversion team must handle and translate 53 attributes every 60 minutes in an eight-hour day. A final sigh escapes when the scope of the challenge was made explicit: Locate, identify, understand, map, transform, document and assure the quality of each attribute at a rate of 0.86 attributes per minute!

This is what we like to refer to as *x-treme data management*, and, of course, the chances of this occurring on time, within budget and with full functionality are exactly zero. What is really amazing is that everyone seems consigned to paying for the overruns. Of course, if you incentivize bad behavior, you shouldn't be surprised when it occurs.

We contacted the previous three clients serviced by the proposed consulting team and found that, on average, the data conversion portion of the last three projects ran over by two years and resulted in more than $3,000,000 dollars in project overruns for the data conversions alone. To conclude this short tale, management pointed out this and other inconsistencies to the consultancy. We offered them a choice: submit a firm, fixed price for the data conversion task or resubmit the bid with more realistic numbers. This produced a vastly revised proposal that resulted in a lower overall total cost structure for the government.

How about measuring before deciding to customize? (If $1 million is substantial)

A second ERP example illustrates how good metadata management practices lead to a better decision-making process with respect to evaluating customization options. Much of this material is an extension of research originally published with our colleague, Lynda Hodgson (Billings, Hodgson et al. 1999).

Initial comparisons of legacy functionality to *new and improved* functionality (most often inappropriately made *after* product selection) indicated that operational processes that had been concisely addressed using a single screen in the legacy system now required operators to mentally integrate information across 23 screens! Faced with the reality of the complexity introduced, one scared executive asked the system integrators to advise as to how big a change was necessary to reverse the ERP's designation of a single data element, PERSON-ID, and revert to a more familiar (but still improper) SSN as the system's primary ID. Of course, the answer came back: *Not a big change at all.*

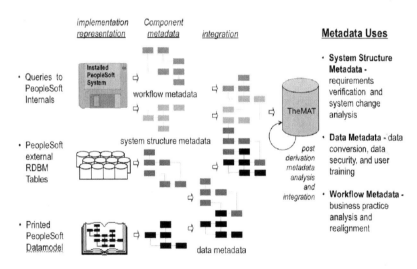

Figure 14   Reverse engineering PeopleSoft's ERP

To quantify that reassuring statement, we accessed our ERP metadata, having reverse-engineered it previously; see Figure 14 and (Aiken, Ngwenyama et al. 1999). This permitted us to understand which ERP components would require alteration in order to re-implement SSN as a centrally accessed data structure throughout the system. Understanding which PROCESSES were connected by PANELS to specific FIELDS, permitted us to identify all of the required modifications (see Figure 15). These included:

- 1,400 ERP panels (display screens);
- 1,500 data tables; and
- 984 business process component steps.

We applied a measure of $200 per hour to a total of 971 hours of labor (assuming 15 minutes required for each change) and came up with a total of at least $200 thousand worth of changes.

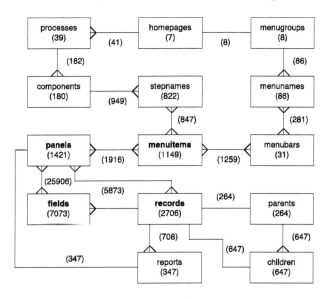

Figure 15   PeopleSoft meta-model

Interestingly, this organization enforced a requirement that the cost of any modification to the new software must be factored into the implementation at a 5X cost. That is, if the cost of modifying the new software was $100 – the organization would add $100 X 5 = $500 to the implementation cost. This was done to provide a disincentive to modify the software.[14]

We wish more organizations would adopt this somewhat unusual but very reasonable practice as it forces organizations to consider that initial required modifications must also be implemented to each subsequent upgrade (in this case, five). This rightly raises the cost of customization to a more realistic amount number and forces organizations to more carefully consider the full cost of proposed modifications.

So, the initial cost (proposed at $200,000) was actually $1 million. This exercise added specific dollar costs to the comment, *Not a big change at all*! When we also pointed out the unreasonableness of assuming 15 minutes per change, the executive withdrew the request.

Is it really that complicated? ($5,500,000 and a person-century of labor savings)

Our third ERP/package software example illustrates how sound data management practices were used to support a hybrid manual-automated solution decision. Based on determining the point of diminishing returns, this final example, to our knowledge, is the first documented, data management savings of a person-century (as opposed to calling it "100 person years").

A large government agency was preparing to implement its ERP. This organization managed over two million stock-keeping units (SKUs) in its catalog. The challenge presented was the existence of master data captured in clear text (also known as comments fields) in the legacy database. The master data arrived there when a previous group of consultants succeeded in getting Oracle, a relational database management system, to act as a hierarchical database management system – *so there would be no need to change related software application processing!* It was widely taken for granted that, because the organization's master data existed in clear text fields, it would have to be *extracted manually*. As an alternative, we introduced an improvable text mining process that converted the non-tabular data into tabular data and verified its correctness against an evolving but verified set of master SKUs.

One of the big questions about improvable solutions is: *when does one achieve good enough?* Or to put it more clearly, how does one determine the point of diminishing returns? The answer is: when the value from additional effort exceeds the cost of the effort. In our solution, a fixed weekly cost was one-half of the weekly salaries of two data engineers conducting the text mining. (One-half salary was used because the engineers were also performing a number of related tasks focused on improving the overall quality of the dataset, and the actual mining process was an hours-long batch run.) By holding the development costs constant (1/2 the weekly salaries), it was possible to discern the relative pay-offs of specific data management driven decisions. The 18-week process is summarized in Figure 16.

	A	B	C	D
1		Unmatched Items	Ignorable Items	Items Matched
2	Week #	(% Total)	(% Total)	(% Total)
3	1	31.47%	1.34%	N/A
4	2	21.22%	6.97%	N/A
5	3	20.66%	7.49%	N/A
6	4	32.48%	11.99%	55.53%
7	...	...	...	...
8	14	9.02%	22.62%	68.36%
9	15	9.06%	22.62%	68.33%
10	16	9.53%	22.62%	67.85%
11	17	9.50%	22.62%	67.88%
12	18	7.46%	22.62%	69.92%

Figure 16   Calculating the point of diminishing returns

The initial goal had been to achieve a 50% reduction in the projected workload facing the team. After the first week, exactly zero items were matched (D3),[15] but the first week's results included identification of more than 26,800 records (or 1.34% of the total) that could be ignored (C3) from this point onward. The

---

[15] Cell identifiers appear within parentheses.

unmatched column (B3) indicated the percentage of the SKUs with no corresponding entry in the master file (31.47%). Over the next four weeks, our scoring of the unmatched items remained largely unchanged (B3 to B6), but the records we could identify as definitively ignorable increased to 11.99% (C6) and—important from a morale perspective—our matching jumped to over 55% (D6).

By the end of week four (row 6), the problem space had been reduced to two-thirds of the original challenge [55% (D6) + 11.99% (C6) = 66.99%], and the question now changed from *Is this a good approach?* To *How long do we continue with this approach?*

Optimization was still an important consideration. To address this question, the chart has been shortened, limiting the presentation of the measurement results to the last four weeks of results (rows 8-12) to show how the team, consisting of both clients and consultants, easily arrived at the decision point. The revised project goal was now *to reduce the manual effort to as little as possible within the original project budget guidelines.* Weekly progress was reviewed by the teams, and accomplishments were noted:

- A decrease in unmatched items from 32% to 7.46% (B6 to B12); meaning that, in real SKU terms, of the original 2 million individual SKUs, only about 150,000 now required manual intervention. The text mining process, along with the automated workflow, addressed 92.5% of the original problem space.
- An increase in the number of ignorable items from just under 11.99% (C6) to 22.62% C12). More than 450,000 SKUs were immediately ignorable, reducing the problem space by more than 20%.
- An increase in the items matched from 55% (D6) to just under 70% (D12). This measurement indicated the successful creation of the resulting, high-value, golden master copy of the item master file.

This outcome permitted calculation of specific values such as *per SKU* and *per person-year*. The project team agreed that only marginal additional value could be achieved after week 18 and, thus, terminated refinement of the text mining at that point. These results were compared against the proposed manual extraction process. For the purposes of comparison, each person-year of effort was valued at $60,000, and the agreed-to total project value is shown in Figure 17.

Time needed to review all NSNs once over the life of the project:	
NSNs	2,000,000
Average time to review & cleanse (in minutes)	5
Total Time (in minutes)	10,000,000
Time available per resource over a one year period of time:	
Work weeks in a year	48
Work days in a week	5
Work hours in a day	7.5
Work minutes in a day	450
Total Work minutes/year	108,000
Person years required to cleanse each NSN once prior to migration:	
Minutes needed	10,000,000
Minutes available person/year	108,000
Total Person-Years	92.6
Resource Cost to cleanse NSN's prior to migration:	
Avg Salary for SME year (not including overhead)	$60,000.00
Projected Years Required to Cleanse/Total DLA Person Year Saved	93
Total Cost to Cleanse/Total DLA Savings to Cleanse NSN's:	$5.5 million

Figure 17   Calculating a person-century of savings

It was agreed that data management had contributed at least a cumulative value of $5.5 million when using a time measure of five minutes (circled on the figure) to review and cleanse each individual data item. Of course such a number was ludicrous, and that precise point was made during presentation of the results. Key, of course, was the observation that, if the time required was doubled to 10 minutes per SKU, it would require 186 person-years; if the time permitted was 15 minutes, it would require 279 person-years to accomplish the task—almost three person-centuries. More importantly, in our experience, very few data quality challenges requiring only 15 minutes to resolve have been encountered.

REAL SOLUTION COST ($30,000,000 VERSUS A ROOMFUL OF MBAS)

On another adventure, we encountered a data warehouse for a healthcare provider. Our entrance into the organization was via the chief financial officer on behalf of the chief executive officer. The CEO wanted an independent evaluation of the project as it had completely overrun its initial budget. Further, the provider had sunk more than $30 million into its development. The dataset was daunting!

- It attempted to completely describe each of the organization's 1.8 million members.
- It contained entries for 1.4 million providers. At this ratio, each provider would provide excellent service for each provider's 1.3 patients. (Yes, 1.3.)
- 800,000 of the providers had no key associated with their records, rendering them practically useless as they were immune to retrieval.
- Only 2.2% of provider records had all of the required nine digits (in a field named PROV_NUMBER), which led to the question, *why is 97% of the data in the warehouse inaccessible?*

The real *coup de grace*, however, was that **the entire warehouse had exactly one operational user**. That's right, just one! And of course the under-resourced area's tardiness in producing required reports triggered the request for the independent evaluation.

"I could have assigned a roomful of MBAs and accomplished this analysis faster!" was the comment heard from the CEO, who, as it happened, was unsympathetic to information technology support for the project.

While it is important not to generalize from small samples, Gartner claims that "more than half of data warehouse/business intelligence projects will have limited acceptance or will be failures through 2013."[16] Of course, in this instance, it was easy to total the costs of these efforts using activity-based costing and other techniques and, with just one user, come up with a total cost of ownership—proving the CEO's previous point.

TWO TANK CASES

The next two cases illustrate challenges around two vastly different types of tanks.

Why are we spending money on stuff we can't even use? ($5 billion)

A friend and colleague, Peter Benson, describes an airplane from a logistics information perspective: "An F-15 is just 171,000 parts flying in very close formation."[17] This statement inspired an investigation by one branch of the Armed Forces. We would soon learn a very interesting fact: each *tank* purchased was really a collection of more than three million data values (Figure 18). And guess how many of those values reflected that the tank was actually obsolete? Well, the challenge was that no one really knew the answer.

Losing track of the significance of tracking materiel obsolescence, as well as the importance of managing the data that described *tank*, wound up costing the Service Branch funding while it spent

---

[16] According to The Data Warehousing Institute http://www.tdwi.eu/home/events/conferences/tdwi-2013-munich/sessiondetails/?tx_mwconferences_pi1%5BshowUid%5D=631&tx_mwconferences_pi1%5Banchor%5D=%23M5P2&tx_mwconferences_pi1%5Bs%5D=0

[17] http://www.slideshare.net/PeterBenson/why-join-eccma-2013-0226

unnecessary funds maintaining expired inventory during a time of war.

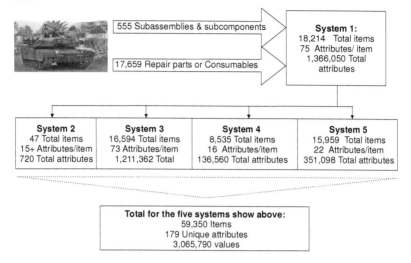

Figure 18   Each tank comprised of 3 million data items

Carrying obsolete tanks generated unnecessary costs and negatively impacted warfighting efforts. Procuring parts for maintenance of obsolete materiel tied up monetary and human resources that could have been put to better and more relevant use. Undefined costs impacted the following operational areas:

- Mission Readiness – resources focused on the non-value-added task of maintaining obsolete inventory, creating constraints on the agency's main mission
- Storage – the costs of physical structures and real estate needed to house items
- Handling – transportation and human resources that were dedicated to moving, maintaining, counting and securing outdated inventory
- Opportunity – inventory that could have been returned to the manufacturer or sold to free up financial assets for more necessary and critical supplies

- Systemic – cost of maintaining inventory information and paper or electronic records which could have been used to support mission-critical acquisitions and distribution
- Equipment Lifecycle Management – cost of maintaining and repairing obsolete items

The errors were discovered using various data analysis technologies that permitted tracking of individual tanks through their respective lifecycles. Application of data profiling resulted in some profound conclusions. We discovered that obsolete equipment literally worth $5 billion was being unnecessarily maintained as a result of poor data management practices. These funds have since been freed up and applied to more direct warfighting missions.

The vocabulary of tanks ($4 million alternative to software package customization)

Tanks were also important to a petroleum products company that made the decision to use an out-of-the-box ERP. It traded increased precision related to various uses of one term, *tank*, within the organization for a projected $4 million cost associated with modifying the ERP. After purchasing, but before installing, the new ERP software, the company discovered that the accounting module counted each transfer of a component from one tank to another tank as a retail transaction! This of course did not meet organizational needs, and they were faced with a dilemma, having only one of four options:

1. Modify existing business practices.
2. Request modifications of the new software – projected cost $4 million.
3. Do some each of option 1 and option 2.
4. Ignore the problem.

Most organizations do not make a formal choice from the above list. In this instance, following analysis, the organization committed to governing the data items so that software could be used without modification. Careful governance of the use of a single term *tank*, and all various sub-types of *tank*, was instituted throughout the organization. Confusing terms (a) would have led to non-sale internal transfers (that is, from one tank to another) being counted as additional retail sales and (b) could have forced the organization to restate its earnings. Now years past the initial decision, the organization calculates that it has saved not just the initial $4 million but subsequent millions annually in software customization and retrofitting costs that would have been required with each subsequent ERP upgrade.

THE ADDITIONAL 45% IS WORTH $50 MILLION[18]

When you pack for a week's vacation in Florida, you follow some simple steps. When you pack for a backpacking trip to Europe, you follow the same simple steps; however, you measure success differently. One success measure for the backpacking trip: everything must fit into backpacks because we must be able to carry them for long periods of time. This success measure is not even considered for a Florida trip.

When our organizations transform to a data-centric approach, we begin to measure success differently than we did before—same project, same process, but with different measures that include:

- asking if our data is correct;
- valuing data more than valuing "on time and within budget;"
- valuing correct data more than correct process; and
- auditing data rather than project documents.

---

[18] This section was authored by Linda Bevolo and edited by the co-authors who are indebted to her for such a substantive and timely contribution.

As we do so, we see a shift as the entire organization begins to speak in terms of data.

While working for a Top 10 financial institution, the technology team was given a project to calculate a new field:

NEW field (E) = A + B/C

where A is sourced from 1 of 6 systems, B is another customer record sourced from 1 of 6 systems, and C is data provided by a vendor.

We planned this project like all others, using our project waterfall methodology and standard software development lifecycle development. As was typical, the team addressed an approved set of business requirements. During development, we identified problem loan records with different fields available for the calculation. Some loans were missing field A, others were missing field B, while others still were missing the vendor-provided value for C. Working within the requirements, we resolved the anomalies identified during development. We reached out to other systems to populate missing fields, and we created new matching routines to grab data from separate loan records. After months of effort and bringing resolution to everything we could, we were finally ready to go to user acceptance testing.

The team was asked one question before approval of the code to migrate to user acceptance testing: *For how many loans were we able to calculate the new field?*
The response: *43%.*

Naturally, the question followed: *Why only 43%?* The response:

We still have bad and missing data. We resolved everything we could. We do not have the required fields populated for all loans; therefore, the calculation does not return a value. We know it sounds low, but we double-checked and all requirements have been satisfied.

As a result, the team was challenged to conduct a deeper dive and provide detailed metrics—not something developers typically do. They met the challenge and produced metrics designed around the missing data. With the deeper dive, we had exact numbers to share with the client. They agreed: *43% did not meet their expectation!* In order to generate more accounts that calculated the NEW Field Calc(E), we collaborated with the client and the vendor. After several iterations, we attained the following results:

1. We received updated business rules from the client to accommodate the "bad data," and we were able to use alternate fields when field A, B or C was blank.
2. We discovered and corrected a code error that caused a zero value in B for a select group of loan records. Field B was populated on many loan records; only a specific group of loans missed the calculation.
3. We identified and had the vendor correct several errors on column C.

Figure 19 displays metrics tracked during rework with the client and the vendor. By the time we deployed to user acceptance testing, we were able to increase the rate of "Computed a valid New Field Calc(E)" from 43 % to 88% and explain every scenario of accounts unable to calculate the new field.

All percentages are computed as a percentages of the total record count

					Breakdown by System of Origination											
					Orig System 1		Orig System 3		Orig System 3		Orig System 4		Acquisition		Unknown	
			Count	Percentage	Count	%	Count	%	Count	%	Count	%	Count	%	Count	%
		Total Records	267,803		60.567	22.616%	16,002	5.975%	22,502	8.402%	13,743	5.132%	7.178	2.680%	147,811	55.194%
		Loans that do not require the NEW Field Calc (E) - per BRD	51,765	19.330%	7,867	2.938%	2,013	0.752%	881	0.329%	1,961	0.732%	1,247	0.466%	37,796	14.113%
		Total Records with Paid in Full records removed	216,038		52,700	24.394%	13,989	6.475%	21,621	10.008%	11,782	5.454%	5.931	2.745%	110,015	50.924%
		Loans that used a default value from Servicing for New Field Calc (E)	5,384	2.492%	5,029	2.328%	303	0.140%	49	0.023%			3	0.001%		
		Computed a valid NEW Field Calc (E)	190,290	88.082%	46,544	21.544%	13,507	6.252%	21,195	9.811%	9,425	4.36%	4,224	1.955%	95,395	44.157%
		Loans unable to calc New Field Calc(E)	20,364	9.426%	1.127	0.522%	179	0.083%	377	0.175%	2,357	1.09%	1.704	0.789%	14,620	6.767%
	SEL	Breakdown of the Zero values														
*	X	Vendor returns a ZERO for Value C	5,179	2.397%	675	0.312%			278	0.129%	2,269	1.050%	1,599	0.740%	358	0.166%
**	X	Vendor returns a NULL for Value C	4,420	2.046%	4	0.002%			6	0.003%			1	0.000%	4,409	2.041%
		No value for A	192	0.089%	9	0.004%			7	0.003%			1	0.000%	175	0.081%
***	x	No value for B	8,449	3.911%	99	0.046%		0.000%	25	0.012%	7	0.003%	35	0.016%	8,283	3.834%
		Invalid value for A	4	0.002%	2	0.001%			1	0.000%		0.000%			1	0.000%
		Invalid value for B	1,319	0.611%	334	0.155%	179	0.083%	60	0.028%	78	0.036%	41	0.019%	627	0.290%
		Invalid value for A + B	750	0.347%	1	0.000%									749	0.347%
		New Field Calc(E) returns BAD value	51	0.024%	3	0.001%		0.000%			3	0.001%	27	0.012%	18	0.008%
		Loans unable to calc New Field Calc(E)	20,364	9.426%	1.127	0.522%	179	0.083%	377	0.175%	2,357	1.091%	1.704	0.789%	14,620	6.767%
		Total Computed with highlighted rows adde	208,338	96.44%												

place an "X" in column B on selected rows to include values in this total

Figure 19 Tracking metrics

Had we completed analysis using our typical project approach, we would have delivered a new, calculated field on 43% of production loans. We would have met all the requirements, passed user acceptance testing and deployed to production. And the project would have been declared a success since we finished on time and under budget.

However, with a data-centric approach and using data to measure success, we were able to increase the number of loan records with the new field from 43% to 88% and enable the client to realize an additional $50 million in savings. This was the result of only *one project* that calculated only *one new field*. Imagine the impact of implementing this approach for all enterprise projects.

WHAT HAPPENED TO OUR FUNDING? (AT LEAST $1 MILLION IN GOVERNMENT FUNDING)

Funding for USAID has traditionally been determined based on personnel head counts. The problem? At one point in their history, USAID did not know how many people actually worked there, primarily because it lacked a standard definition for *employee*. This led to conflicting statements such as in 2009 when it was:

- reported to the White House that they had 10,000;
- reported to Congress that they had 11,000 employees; and
- eventually determined, after a review of Microsoft licenses in an attempt to clarify these discrepancies was undertaken, more than 15,000 licenses existed.

If the cost of underreporting personnel head counts was only $1,000/employee, the organization was missing more than $1 million annually. Missing out on funding due to a lack of quality data management also highlighted other important operational impacts: inaccuracy regarding just exactly who is employed and the qualifications of actual employees. In crisis situations, USAID must be able to respond quickly and send the right people to the right place at the right time, but a resulting lack of adequate funding prevented development of systems (such as one prototype shown as Figure 20) that better support USAID's mission.

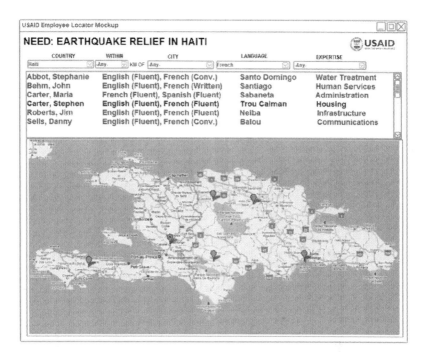

Figure 20   USAID prototype screen

BUT DATA STUFF IS COMPLICATED; HOW DO I EXPLAIN IT? (£500 REALLY INCREASED PROJECT CLARITY)

One of the most difficult tasks with any data related initiative is that of explaining (or, as it is more commonly known, *selling*) the project. In one of the most articulate examples witnessed, a group at BT (formerly British Telecom) created the animation below to educate everyone in the entire company about its master data management initiative known as Seven Sisters. With permission, we've selectively illustrated a copy of this gem in Figure 21 (posted on the Web at: http://www.datablueprint.com/aiken-book-monetizing-data-management.

Figure 21   A small investment in a visual explanation of the technical approach

Take a minute to watch it. For a very small investment, BT was able to hire talent that quite articulately transferred the entire dialog into a 44-second message; it was a bit of fun as well. The entire text of the Flash™ presentation follows. "Previously information was stored in hundreds of databases across BT. Processes were duplicated. Effort was wasted. It was all a bit messy. Now we are sorting all of our data—making it much easier to deal with."

The animation closed with a pictorial description of data being sorted into seven piles so clearly laid out that non-information technology staff was able to identify a number of the desired master data management stacks. This small investment of a few British pounds proved the beginning of an invaluable communication channel and set the bar high with respect to communications coming from information technology.

Chapter 3
Real Live Pay-offs: Five Non-Monetary Cases

The first non-monetary case concerns improved decision-making and the second an issue of national security. The others involve saving lives. All concern C-level decision makers.

DETERMINING OBJECTIVE SELECTION CRITERIA FOR LEGACY SYSTEM CONSOLIDATION (AND AVOIDING A CONGRESSIONAL INQUIRY IN THE PROCESS)

The first author was employed by the Defense Information Systems Agency during the early 1990s. One of the first conversations he had with his boss' boss began with her stating: "Your task is to keep me from having to testify in front of a congressional inquiry!" To a newbie federal government employee, this was an unpromising start. It seemed that the DISA Center for Information Management had been tasked with developing recommendations regarding Department of Defense payroll systems. At the time, there were 37 payroll systems generating payments to civilian employees. Both the number of systems and upcoming preparation for Y2K were putting pressure on the department to simplify its environment.

In addition to the number of systems, more profound data-related challenges were revealed. Various individuals, in their attempts to determine the total number of civilians employed by the department, submitted comprehensive requests for the individual systems to report regarding items such as number of employees covered. The inevitable rejoinder from each system was something like: *"What do you mean by employee?"* followed by *"This is how we define it for our system."*

While it might have seemed impertinent, the question was quite reasonable. Since each system defined *employee* (a very important Master Data concept) differently, each request from headquarters had to be further qualified so that the "real" count be determined. For example, does the request pertain to just full-time or does it also include part-time employees? That systems used different definitions was due to a lack of data standards within the department.

There was a subordinate, theoretically unnecessary cost resulting from the lack of standardization as well. The actual (and, more importantly, perceived) cost of answering what appeared to be a simple question was high as a result of the time required to manually reconcile the disparate data required to standardize responses. For example, if a given system returned the total number of full- and part-time employees, then the number of part-time employees had to be manually subtracted from the overall total if the initial query pertained only to full-time employees.

This arrangement presented a secondary challenge as it preserved the status quo. In spite of valiant efforts by the participants, not only was virtually every request frustrating to satisfy, the data comprising the response was inevitably of poor quality as well— which contributed to poor quality decision-making. Many initial requests for DoD-wide information went unsatisfied as the frustrating cost of clarifying the initial (seemingly reasonable) request grew to unreasonable proportions. So, efforts to improve operations were actually hampered by poor departmental data management practices.

Back to the challenge. The request for recommendations was clearly motivated by a desire to reduce the number of departmental civilian pay systems needed—ideally to just one. The effort was to involve a study and recommendations regarding which system to keep and how to merge all others into the surviving system. Because the 37 systems were located in 37 states, local congressional delegations, anxious to demonstrate unique capabilities of each system and to convince the study team of the virtues of each (as well as anxious to preserve local jobs), invited the team to visit on-site and personally inspect the various systems.

It quickly became apparent that, with the desired outcome being a single system to perform all DoD civilian payroll processing, there would be 36 losing systems (or 37 losers if the decision was to merge all 37 into a new system). With so many potential losers, a daunting congressional inquiry seemed inevitable. What was clearly needed was a means to objectively compare the 37 systems against departmental requirements. Newbie's boss' boss was also aware that a previous process modeling exercise for each system had produced thoroughly uninteresting and non-helpful results: each system was virtually indistinguishable from the other 36 systems – from a process perspective. After all, how much variation can a payroll process exhibit and still comply with organizational processing standards?

The method designed was eventually documented in DoD-mandated instruction (Aiken 1996). It permitted objective evaluation and comparison of the systems using data reverse-engineering to determine data types processed by each system. This made it possible to determine that the system in Florida supported maintenance of more departmental data requirements than another system because it included requirements similar to the following: *One-legged engineers + working in waist deep water + under rotating helicopter blades + on overtime.*

When congressional delegations from the various "losing" systems inquired as to the reasons their systems were not selected, the "one-legged engineer" example was often enough to satisfy their questions. The feared congressional inquiry never materialized, and the department was able to begin planning system consolidation with minimal fuss.

Data migration planning was based directly on metadata discovered during the study and was several times less expensive than originally anticipated as a result. The department saved millions as a result of simplified processing, reduced technology footprints and economies of scale. More importantly, the department was finally able to answer specific questions now that it possessed a single source of standardized data.

Interestingly, no one attempted to calculate the cost of implementing standardized data and avoiding the cost of systems consolidation.

EVERYONE HAS BILLS TO PAY (BUT SOME BILLS ARE MORE EQUAL THAN OTHERS)

The Pentagon contracts for services with many service providers and, consequently, processes many, many invoices. When this data management challenge evolved over time and was not engineered (or periodically re-engineered) for optimal performance, processing slowed and, on occasion, halted. The result? Invoices did not get paid. On the other side of the accounting equation, when service providers do not get paid for services previously rendered, a natural response is to halt further services. And when the service in question is responsible for providing Internet connectivity to the Pentagon, consequences can be enormous.

The operational unit responsible for utilizing the accounting system shared by Pentagon operations and other DoD organizations often encountered poor system reliability and, as a result, relied heavily on manual processing. Things came to a head when the Pentagon's Internet connection was almost turned off as a result of unpaid invoices for service. The threat to the Pentagon of losing Internet connectivity provided the motivation necessary to identify and quantify opportunities to improve data quality, entry and reporting. We were called in to develop the plan and deliver results quickly with better reporting practices, permitting the service provider to identify "important" accounts. A data centric fix let the billing company assign a flag to the various accounts indicating that automatic cut off procedures should not apply to flagged accounts.

Can an anywhere-near-accurate monetary value be assigned when the Pentagon is unable to access the Internet specifically as a result of poor data management resulting in poorly designed bill processing on the part of the Pentagon's internet provider?

IDENTIFYING PAYMENT ERROR CORRECTION AND BOOSTING TROOP MORALE? (PRICELESS)

And speaking of payroll, please help us place a true value on a compensation payment error—especially a compensation error occurring over multiple years to an army private who is serving his county under warfighting conditions. First, one must ask: *What is the actual cost of diverting the attention of not just the warfighter, but also, in this instance, a private's lieutenant, also under fire, who is concerned with correcting a four-year compensation underpayment for one of his soldiers?* In this case, it cannot be accomplished easily or in a straightforward manner.

For a private in the armed services, experiencing greater need for immediate cash management than a higher-ranking member of the military, a pay issue can be critical to the wellbeing of family members. Moreover, pay issues represent negative impact to troop and unit morale, focus and mission outcomes. Brig. Richard Nugee, in his keynote address at the 2010 Data Governance Conference, reported that the actual time to resolve just such an issue took many, many hours over a period of months to correct a processing error that resulted in underpayment of approximately $12 thousand (Nugee and Seiner 2010). The reported cause of the issue was a rather simple data management issue; bad quality data was originally input to the system. Good quality data management processes would have prevented the poor quality data from entering the system instead of allowing the individual who entered the data to believe that it had been done correctly. Data governance principles encouraging the prevention of incorrect data to be entered into the payroll system would have mandated the design and implementation of upfront checking instead of attempting to validate data items after initial input.

To quantify the cost of the example presented, we can (1) total the number of hours for respective time spent by the two individuals addressing the issue and (2) multiply these hours by their hourly pay rates. The lowest active private annual pay rate in the British Armed Forces is approximately $27 thousand, while the lowest annual pay rate for a lieutenant is approximately $38 thousand.[19] In fiscal terms, it would take only a small investment of their time to exceed the cost of resolving the underpayment error. However, there is simply no way to include non-quantifiable costs associated with this situation in the final total because we cannot precisely quantify the presumably negative value of the situational impact to individual and unit morale, loss of focus and mission outcome.

Horrifyingly but realistically, the true cost of either individual's diversion may be a fatality. Most certainly, it makes no sense for the cost of the correction to have exceeded the cost of the adjustment. Unfortunately, at this point of maturity in the data management profession, there is no toolset that permits precise identification of the *total costs* of this data management error. With practice, we can get better but, so far, outside of Brig. Nugee's unit, this skill has not been recognized as necessary, so very few practitioners or researchers are exploring it.

---

[19] http://www.armedforces.co.uk/armypayscales.htm

SAVING WARFIGHTER LIVES (FRIENDLY FIRE DEATH PREVENTION)

The story below, posted to an on-line forum often visited to follow discussions regarding computer risk,[20] is, unfortunately not an isolated tale. Based on keen interest in the role played by data in these types of incidents, it has become apparent that the issue is of growing importance. The story posted to the forum is below.

Date: Tue, 26 Mar 2002 10:47:52 -0500
From: Subject: Friendly Fire deaths traced to dead battery

In one of the more horrifying incidents I've read about, U.S. soldiers and allies were killed in December 2001 because of a stunningly poor design of a GPS receiver, plus "human error."
http://www.washingtonpost.com/wp-dyn/articles/A8853-2002Mar23.html

A U.S. Special Forces air controller was calling in GPS positioning from some sort of battery-powered device. He "had used the GPS receiver to calculate the latitude and longitude of the Taliban position in minutes and seconds for an airstrike by a Navy F/A-18." According to the *Post* story, the bomber crew "required" a "second calculation in 'degree decimals'" -- why the crew did not have equipment to perform the minutes-seconds conversion themselves is not explained. The air controller had recorded the correct value in the GPS receiver when the battery died. Upon replacing the battery, he called in the degree-decimal position the unit was showing -- without realizing that the unit is set up to reset to its *own* position when the battery is replaced. The 2,000-pound bomb landed on his position, killing three Special Forces soldiers and injuring 20 others. If the information in this story is accurate, the RISKS involve replacing memory settings with an

---

[20] http://catless.ncl.ac.uk/Risks

apparently-valid default value instead of blinking 0 or some other obviously-wrong display; not having a backup battery to hold values in memory during battery replacement; not equipping users to translate one coordinate system to another; and using a device with such flaws in a combat situation.

The very idea that any contractor would sell to the US Armed Forces a device that, when replacing the batteries, would reset a target to a soldier's own position without sufficient warning is inconceivable. While it would seem to incorporate a broadly focused discussion on product development lifecycles and approaches, here we are concerned with good data management practices which always dictate that alerts related to recently changed positions are not only standard in modern operating systems, but also expected by the users of today's smart phone apps!

SAVING WARFIGHTER LIVES (US ARMY SUICIDE PREVENTION: A CLEAR DATA GOVERNANCE SUCCESS)

We were fortunate to play a small role in support of the Army's suicide prevention efforts and, at one point, made a significant contribution. As part of the effort, extensive and detailed coordination was needed to manage project-critical data from a variety of organizations. Diagrams (such as Figure 22) were considered key to coordinating the various data requests.

Time deadlines were tight; we needed to make the various coordination meetings as efficient and effective as possible. While all the participating organizations wanted to support such a good cause, *"Our data is bound by certain terms and conditions..."* was a phrase repeated over and over again. Worse, the condition was interpreted as a need for more analysis and discussion. This, of course, required the one resource that we were lacking: time.

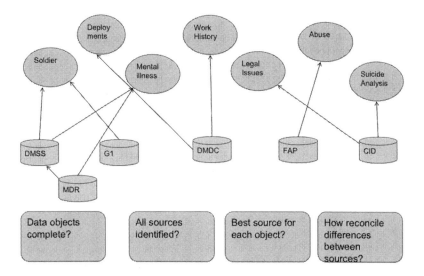

Figure 22   Attempted mapping of sources and uses of data

A meeting was arranged wherein all involved data stewards were gathered. Also invited to this meeting was Thomas E. Kelly III, then Deputy Under-Secretary of the U.S. Army, the senior officer, who, after repeatedly hearing the phrase, "my data," reminded all present that the data actually belonged to the senior officer since all present reported to him through the existing chain of command. Immediately following this reminder, the phrase, "my data," was banished from the group's vocabulary, except when referring to the senior officer's data. The reminder was issued tactfully but with enough force to carry the weight of an order.

At the end of the meeting, the senior officer reiterated the process for handling questions as to future data ownership: "Make an appointment to speak directly with me!" This single event, known in information technology circles as executive buy-in, served several purposes, all of which saved valuable time in the effort to prevent future soldier suicides. By agreeing to take command of the data, the senior officer provided a very heavy dose of management support for the project.

If all CEOs would take similar direct action and responsibility, there would be an immediate positive impact to the bottom line of their organizations. It would save millions (and, for some organizations, billions) annually.

Perhaps most important, however, was the inherent empowerment of the team. The conversation turned immediately from *Can this be done?* to *How are we going to accomplish this?*

Deputy Under-Secretary Kelly also made clear the need for speed and that mistakes along the way would be tolerated. A perfect solution was not essential; instead, a workable solution in prototype form was acceptable, as it would provide lessons learned while an improved, permanent version was implemented. This case in particular demonstrates how an act of data governance management increased the speed at which a prototype solution was developed!

Chapter 4
And Then There Are the Lawyers:
An Illustrative Legal Matter

Most information technology projects are governed by contracts that assign responsibilities to each party and provide specific legal remedies for delayed implementation or project failure. Because data is typically involved in all information technology projects, the potential impact of such constraints is huge.

DISTINCT INCENTIVES: DATA MANAGEMENT SAVES LEGAL COSTS

In formal court proceedings, court costs can be assessed and assigned but, in many cases, outsourced information technology project contracts now require the parties to submit to private, binding arbitration to resolve disputes. Arbitration agreements, however, heavily favor contractors because of additional costs to the client associated with arbitration—not to mention outright legal costs. As a result, far too many consultants get away with poor performance because the client doesn't have the stomach to fund the cost of the legal action required to hold the contractors to their advertised service levels.

We have been employed over the years in various capacities to provide expert witness support related to legal disputes. In our opinion, far too often, excessive costs force a client to settle for far less than that to which they are truly entitled. However, in legal disputes, the court system can impose standards, such as those propagated by the IEEE (pronounced, I triple E; the Institute of Electrical and Electronics Engineers), on the performance of such contracts. So, for starters, organizations should seriously rethink acceptance of standard arbitration clauses common in today's information technology contracts.

Let us describe a situation related to conversion from a legacy system to a state-of-the-market enterprise resource planning (ERP) tool. Much of the material comes from an article we wrote for *IEEE Computer* wherein an important development was described regarding the use of standards by which information technology contracts and contractor performance were being evaluated (Aiken, Billings et al. 2010). The article relates how the court system imposed standards, such as those propagated by the IEEE, on information technology projects in arbitration—*and this is really important*—where none of the parties are affiliated with the IEEE. All names are fictitious for obvious reasons.

Company X received a directive from its parent corporation mandating replacement of its legacy payroll and personnel systems with a specific ERP software package designed to standardize payroll and personnel processing enterprise-wide. Upon the vendor's recommendation of a "specialist" integrator, Company X contracted with the recommended specialist to implement the new system and convert its legacy data for $1 million.

The contracted timeline was six months, beginning in July and wrapping up with a "big bang" conversion at the end of December. The year-end conversion failed, allegedly due to the system integrator's poor data migration practices. It became necessary for Company X to run both the old and new systems in parallel—a complex and expensive situation which could have been avoided, and one that Company Y had assured would not occur. When conversion was pushed into April of the following year, Company X slowed and then ceased paying invoices from the system integrator. In July, the system integrator pulled its implementation team, and Company X initiated arbitration. The messy sequencing toward arbitration is shown in Figure 23.

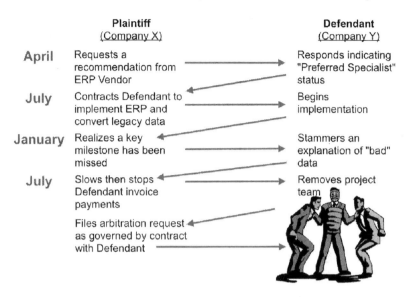

	Plaintiff (Company X)	**Defendant** (Company Y)
April	Requests a recommendation from ERP Vendor	Responds indicating "Preferred Specialist" status
July	Contracts Defendant to implement ERP and convert legacy data	Begins implementation
January	Realizes a key milestone has been missed	Stammers an explanation of "bad" data
July	Slows then stops Defendant invoice payments	Removes project team
	Files arbitration request as governed by contract with Defendant	

Figure 23   Messy sequencing towards arbitration

Note: every contract we have seen has a clause similar, if not identical, to the one in this instance:

[Company Y] warrants that the services it provides hereunder will be performed in a professional and workmanlike manner in accordance with industry standards.

Precisely defining these standards (such as "professional and workmanlike manner") would quickly become a key issue. While providing expert witness testimony in the arbitration proceedings, we were asked to address six specific items of contention, each with its origins in data management, although only issue #3 (data quality) would have been recognized as a data management issue at the time.

Issue #1: Who owned the risks?

Interestingly, at a project kick-off meeting, data quality was one of four project risks that were classified as *high*. Yet when asked why Company Y was unable to meet their own self-imposed deadline, their only response was that 'Company X had *bad data*.' If the potential quality of the data was identified early on as a high risk, who was obligated to develop the risk mitigation plan and monitor for risk occurrence? As Company Y had self-labeled themselves experts, the arbiters indicated a belief that the consultants owned this risk; this was backed up by demonstrating to the arbiters that the DMBOK shows that data quality was clearly a data management issue and therefore the risk belonged to Company Y.

Issue #2: Who was the project manager?

Believe it or not, the system integrator had the client's chief information officer sign a contract stating that Company Y's consultants were working under the CIO's personal direction as the project manager! This document was shown to the arbitration panel; it turned out to be a rather poor move. The arbiters questioned the system integrator as to how, if Company X had hired "experts," would they have been able to direct the work of Company Y's expert consultants? Since the arbiters asked the question directly of the system integrator's representative, proceedings began with the system integrator on a defensive footing--without us having to do any work.

How did data management play a role in this? First, we used the PMBOK, the *Project Management Institute Body of Knowledge*, a) to define what project managers do and b) to identify evidence of those behaviors on the parts of both defendant and plaintiff (see Figure 24). Second, we introduced time and attendance records for one expert consultant who billed more than two thousand hours to a task labeled "project management." Both pieces of evidence were obtained by reverse-engineering the data we obtained as evidence from Company Y's consultant shared drive, where all the project documentation was stored during the project. Needless to say, we won this point handily.

Process area	Defendant lead		Plaintiff
	Methodology	Demonstrated	lead
Scope planning	✓	✓	
Scope definition	✓	✓	
Activity definition	✓	✓	
Activity sequencing	✓	✓	
Activity duration estimation	✓	✓	
Schedule development	✓	✓	
Resource planning	✓	✓	
Cost estimating	✓	✓	
Cost budgeting	✓	✓	
Project plan development	✓	✓	
Quality planning	✓	✓	?
Communication planning	✓	✓	
Risk identification	✓	✓	✓
Risk quantification	✓	✓	
Risk response development	✓	✓	?
Organizational planning	✓	✓	
Staff acquisition	✓	✓	

Figure 24   Establishing who the project manager was

Issue #3: Was the data of poor quality?

A fundamental mistake made when organizations hand over data conversion or migration tasks ("modification") to consultants is the failure to conduct a baseline comparison of data quality before it is turned over. Organizations that forego this simple task are generally defenseless against allegations that a) the data is of poor quality and b) the poor quality inhibited successful modification. On the plus side, organizations performing such basic comparisons are better equipped to evaluate various proposals. In fact, organizations without this basic knowledge cannot make informed responses to such proposed plans or scenarios. Neither party can, in short, have an intelligent, useful conversation because a lack of project-specific information is a necessary albeit insufficient precondition to determining how long it will take and how much the conversion will cost.

The only defense when faced with this challenge is to investigate the possibility that modification activities introduced errors. We were able to offer defense in two instances, one micro and one macro.

Introducing micro errors into conversion data

We found a number of instances such as the one described below. When added together, it painted a picture of errors being introduced into the data by Company Y. Showing that Company Y's conversion made the data worse—regardless of its condition before being handed over—was a pretty good refutation that the original data was of poor quality.

Example: When converting gender information, the system integrator introduced code that basically read as follows:

```
IF column 1 in source = "m" then set value of
target data to "male"
ELSE set value of target data to "female"
```

This code is implemented in direct contradiction to IEEE programming standards, among others. Use of such modification programming code introduces errors into the target because values not equal to "m" in the source will be counted as "female" in the destination. This should not *always* be the case, as there are exceptions to every rule. For example, according to Canadian law at the time, the government mandated the tracking of nine gender codes:

1. Male
2. Female
3. Formerly male now female
4. Formerly female now male
5. Uncertain

6. Won't tell
7. Doesn't know
8. Male soon to be female
9. Female soon to be male

All other values were counted as female after conversion by Company Y's code. Demonstrably, the converted data was of poorer quality than the original, unconverted data as the number of females was incorrectly higher in the converted data.

Introducing macro errors by converting too much data

Our examination of converted data indicated that an order of magnitude more data existed in the target data set than was expected – the source dataset was one-tenth the size of the converted dataset. Our forensics discovered that, when the data didn't "go in right," Company Y's consultant would rerun the conversion process. However, the ERP manufacturer had implemented code that prevented duplicate records from being created within the database. When the rerun also produced unsatisfactory results, the consultants located and disabled the code that prevented duplicate records from being introduced. They then ran the process multiple times (apparently 10), causing the data set to contain multiple duplicate records, resulting in significant dilution of existing data quality.

Once again, the conversion data was of demonstrably lower quality because it contained approximately 10 entries for each entry in the original, legacy data set. For example, a single legacy entry for "Jane Smith" in the original, unconverted data set typically resulted in 10 entries for "Jane Smith" in the migration data set. Each error in the original data was multiplied by 10 times by the conversion process, clearly indicating that Company Y's conversion process had generated data of poorer quality than the unconverted data.

These macro and micro examples clearly demonstrated to the arbiters that the modification process had introduced errors into the data and, thus, the system integrator's claim of poor quality data as the cause of failed data conversion became suspect.

Issue #4: Did the contractor (Company Y) exercise due diligence?

Our expert report introduced dozens of additional forensic artifacts used as project plans at one or more points during the project. Project planning is a basic approach to executing large complex tasks such as a system conversion. Project plans are used to keep everyone involved on the same page as to what is supposed to happen (and when) and what has happened so far during the project.

These project plans were not of the standard variety. Of particular note was the number of tasks constrained by predecessor tasks relative to the total number of tasks in each version of the project plans. In the most egregious example, a total of only 15 of 499 total tasks had predecessors. If this were truly the case, it would not matter when the remaining 484 tasks were begun (Figure 25).

Subdirectory	File name	Last date saved	Total tasks	Tasks with predecessors
Project_Plan\Backup		10/2/20	210	9
Project_Plan\Backup		10/15/2	214	9
Project_Plan		11/17/2	264	0
Project_Plan		11/18/2	262	0
Project_Plan		12/2/20	274	0
Rodolphe		12/2/20	274	0
Rodolphe		12/2/20	0	0
Project_Plan		1/27/20	0	0
Project_Plan		2/23/20	424	3
Project_Plan		2/26/20	425	3
Project_Plan		3/22/20	438	3
Project_Plan		3/22/20	438	3
Project_Plan		4/19/20	470	3
Project_Plan		5/11/20	485	15
Project_Plan		5/13/20	493	15
Project_Plan		5/18/20	499	15
Project_Plan		6/16/20	125	12

Figure 25   Alleged project management plans

The absurdity of these "plans" called into question the project management qualifications of Company Y. They clearly showed that Company Y's consultants were not good at managing the project data. They hadn't a clue how to manage the metadata, *the data about the data,* they were charged with managing.

The contrast between expected and actual behavior was highlighted using guidance from the previously mentioned PMBOK. It clearly showed that the consultants from Company Y were not competent to perform the duties to which they had been assigned. It further established in the mindset of arbiters an equivalency between PMBOK and the DMBOK.

Issue #5: Was Company Y's approach adequate?

Data engineering, like most forms of engineering, establishes specific techniques and principles upon which its practitioners rely (see Figure 26). Most fundamental are the concepts of flexibility, adaptability and reusability. Data engineering methods permit discovery and modeling of the best "to-be" arrangement of the data—the data architecture required to best satisfy the organizational requirements.

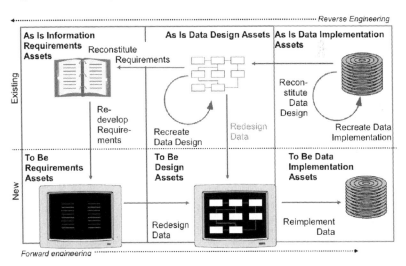

Figure 26   Lacking data reverse-engineering methods

A thorough examination of publicly available documentation of the system integrator's methods revealed no instance even suggesting that such ideal data architecture would be defined. Moreover, upon questioning, none the consulting staff appeared to understand its fundamental importance. The arbiters were left sensing that the system integrator's method was lacking in key areas—namely, defining an adequate "target" arrangement of the data that could satisfy Company X's data needs.

Issue #6: Were required standards of care followed, and were work products of the required quality?

When deciding these various issues, the arbiters returned to the matter of the definition of *standard of care* that could be expected by the client of the contractors. After all, the consultants had promised in writing that the work would be done according to "industry standards." During discovery, a few pointed questions were posed to Company Y's consultants about these standards. The answers below were typical.

> **Question:** What are the industry standards that you are referring to?
>
> **Answer:** There is nothing written or codified, but it is the standards which are recognized by the consulting firms in our industry.
>
> **Question:** I understand from what you told me just a moment ago that the industry standards that you are referring to here are not written down anywhere; is that correct?
>
> **Answer:** That is my understanding.
>
> **Question:** Have you made an effort to locate these industry standards and have simply not been able to do so?
>
> **Answer:** I would not know where to begin to look.

At this point, we were able to convince the arbiters that, absent other sources, Google would not be an unreasonable place to begin. We demonstrated the ease of locating the IEEE standards and then used those standards to contrast with the performance and actions of the consultants. The arbiters were favorably impressed and, in the absence of the referenced best practices, allowed the application of the IEEE standards even though none of the consultants (or the client, for that matter) was a member of the IEEE.

The upshot was that the arbiters sided with our expert opinion and awarded millions to the client. Approaching the entire problem from a data management perspective afforded us unique insight to defend against the poor data quality charge, but it was our related forensics that revealed the various other items of evidence that led to a successful outcome for our client.

Conclusion
Your Charge

We have illustrated that, with a bit of practice; data managers (and other interested parties) can put the cost of poor, and the payoff of good, data management practices into terms that are spoken in the executive suite— most often, money. We have also shown that it is possible to bring the same relevance to other data management pay-offs, whether they are non-monetary (saving lives) or information technology disaster avoidant (legal).

Regardless of the specific monetization focus, all data-centric perspectives will refocus information technology success criteria by:

- asking if our data is correct,
- valuing data more than we value "on time and within budget,"
- appreciating correct data more than correct processes, and
- auditing data rather than project documents.

As we do so, we will see a shift wherein the entire organization begins to speak in terms of *data*.[21] Practicing these can only help your organization's individual data management efforts. Now that you understand data management and how it can be spoken of in terms that others at the corporate chief level can relate to, the rest is up to you.

---

[21] This specific articulation of the data centric perspective comes from the author of Section 0, Linda Bevolo, to whom we are indebted for its conciseness and focus.

References

Aiken, P. H. (1996). Data Reverse Engineering: Slaying the Legacy Dragon. New York, McGraw-Hill.

Aiken, P. H., et al. (2007). "Measuring Data Management Pratice Maturity: A Community's Self-Assessment." IEEE Computer 40(4): 8.

Aiken, P. H., et al. (2010). "Use of the IEEE Codes of Conduct to Resolve Legal Disputes." IEEE Computer 43(4): 5.

Aiken, P. H., et al. (2011). "Data Management and Data Administration: Assessing 25 Years of Practice." Journal of Database Management 22(3): 20.

Aiken, P. H. and M. Gorman (2013). The Case for the Chief Data Officer: Recasting the C-Suite to Leverage Your Most Valuable Asset. San Francisco, Morgan Kaufmann.

Aiken, P. H., et al. (1994). "DoD Legacy Systems: Reverse Engineering Data Requirements." Communications of the ACM 37(5): 15.

Aiken, P. H., et al. (1999). "Reverse Engineering New Systems for Smooth Implementation." IEEE Software 16(2): 36-43.

Appleton, D. (1986). Information Asset Management. Datamation. Newton, MA, Cahners Publishing Company 32: 6.

Billings, J., et al. (1999). The BRIDGE: A Toolkit Approach to Reverse Engineering System Metadata in Support of Migration to Enterprise Software. Advances in Conceptual Modeling ER'99 Workshop on Reverse Engineering in Information Systems, Paris, France, Springer-Verlag, Berlin.

DAMA-International (2009). The Guide to the Data Management Body of Knowledge, Technics Publications, LLC.

Nugee, R. and R. S. Seiner (2010, 6/1/2010). "TDAN.com Interview with Brigadier Richard Nugee – The British Army." 2013, from http://www.tdan.com/view-special-features/13897 and personal communications.

Made in the USA
Middletown, DE
31 July 2018